Maths
made easy

Key Stage 2 upper
ages 9-11
Fractions

Authors

Peter Gash and David Clemson

LONDON • NEW YORK • SYDNEY • DELHI

Eighths

When you divide something into eighths, you share it equally between eight.

Each part, or fraction, is called one eighth. ⟶ [shaded diagram]
You can also write it as $\frac{1}{8}$.

Two parts are two eighths or $\frac{2}{8}$.
Three parts are three eighths or $\frac{3}{8}$, and so on.

Write the fractions for the shaded squares.

Eighths

Write the fractions for the shaded squares.

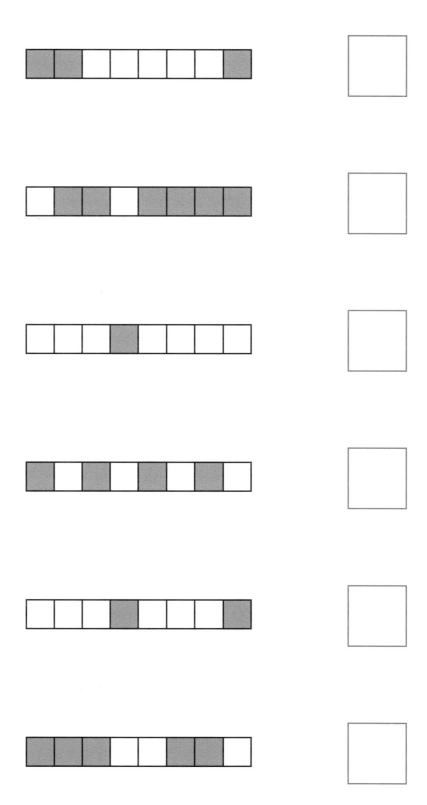

Equivalent fractions

Here are four strips of paper. They are all the same length. Each one has been cut into different fractions. You can see that some fractions are the same. For example, ½ is the same as ²⁄₄.

one whole 1							
½				½			
¼		¼		¼		¼	
⅛	⅛	⅛	⅛	⅛	⅛	⅛	⅛

Look at the strips of paper above. Write the fractions that match.

½ is the same as /8   ¼ is the same as /8

¾ is the same as /8   ²⁄₈ is the same as /4

²⁄₄ is the same as /8   ²⁄₄ is the same as /2

⁶⁄₈ is the same as /4   ½ is the same as /4

Sixths

When you divide something into sixths, you share it equally between six.

Each part, or fraction, is called one sixth. ⟶
You can also write it as $\frac{1}{6}$.

Two parts are two sixths or $\frac{2}{6}$.
Three parts are three sixths or $\frac{3}{6}$, and so on.

Write the fractions for the shaded squares.

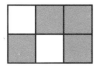

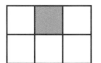

Shade the squares to show the fractions.

$\frac{2}{6}$ $\frac{1}{6}$

$\frac{4}{6}$ $\frac{6}{6}$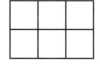

Equivalent fractions

Here are four strips of paper. They are all the same length. Each one has been cut into different fractions. You can see that some fractions are the same. For example, ½ is the same as ³⁄₆.

one whole 1					
½			½		
⅓		⅓		⅓	
⅙	⅙	⅙	⅙	⅙	⅙

Look at the strips of paper above. Write the fractions that match.

⁴⁄₆ is the same as   /3   ⅓ is the same as   /6

1 is the same as   /6   ³⁄₆ is the same as   /2

²⁄₆ is the same as   /3   ⅔ is the same as   /6

½ is the same as   /6   1 is the same as   /2

Fifths

When you divide something into fifths, you share it equally between five.

Each part, or fraction, is called one fifth.
You can also write it as $\frac{1}{5}$.

Two parts are two fifths or $\frac{2}{5}$.
Three parts are three fifths or $\frac{3}{5}$, and so on.

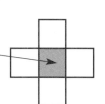

Write the fractions for the shaded shapes.

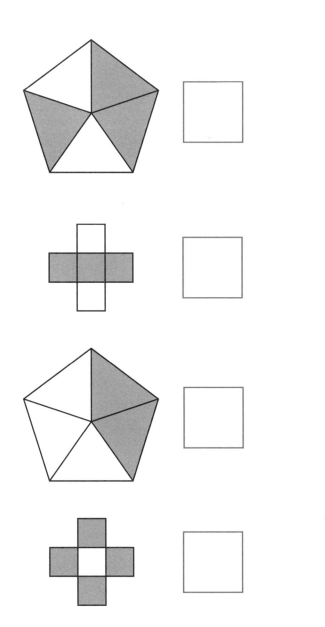

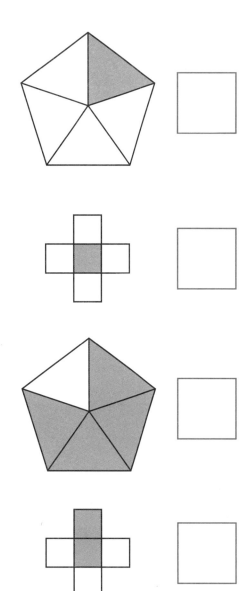

7

Tenths

When you divide something into tenths, you share it equally between ten.

Each part, or fraction, is called one tenth.
You can also write it as $\frac{1}{10}$.

Two parts are two tenths or $\frac{2}{10}$.
Three parts are three tenths or $\frac{3}{10}$, and so on.

Write the fractions for the shaded squares.

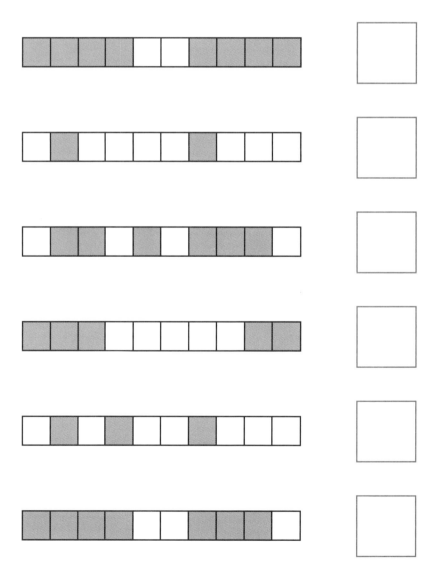

Twentieths

When you divide something into twentieths, you share it equally between twenty.

Each part, or fraction, is called one twentieth.
You can also write it as $\frac{1}{20}$.

Two parts are two twentieths or $\frac{2}{20}$.
Three parts are three twentieths or $\frac{3}{20}$, and so on.

Write the fractions for the shaded squares.

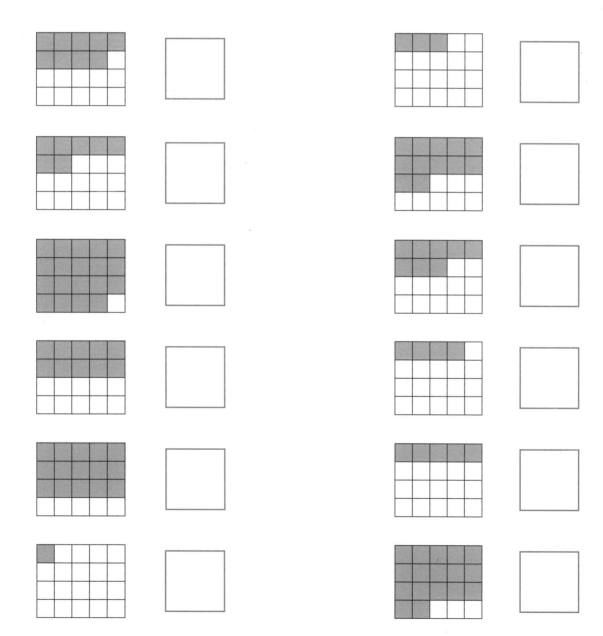

Equivalent fractions

Here are five strips of paper. They are all the same length. Each one has been cut into different fractions. You can see that some fractions are the same. For example, $\frac{1}{2}$ is the same as $\frac{5}{10}$.

one whole 1									
$\frac{1}{2}$					$\frac{1}{2}$				
$\frac{1}{4}$		$\frac{1}{4}$		$\frac{1}{4}$			$\frac{1}{4}$		
$\frac{1}{10}$	$\frac{1}{10}$	$\frac{1}{10}$	$\frac{1}{10}$	$\frac{1}{10}$	$\frac{1}{10}$	$\frac{1}{10}$	$\frac{1}{10}$	$\frac{1}{10}$	$\frac{1}{10}$
$\frac{1}{20}$ $\frac{1}{20}$ $\frac{1}{20}$ $\frac{1}{20}$ $\frac{1}{20}$ $\frac{1}{20}$ $\frac{1}{20}$ $\frac{1}{20}$ $\frac{1}{20}$ $\frac{1}{20}$ $\frac{1}{20}$ $\frac{1}{20}$ $\frac{1}{20}$ $\frac{1}{20}$ $\frac{1}{20}$ $\frac{1}{20}$ $\frac{1}{20}$ $\frac{1}{20}$ $\frac{1}{20}$ $\frac{1}{20}$									

Look at the strips of paper in the box above. Write the fractions that match.

$\frac{2}{4}$ is the same as $\boxed{/10}$

$\frac{2}{4}$ is the same as $\boxed{/20}$

$\frac{4}{10}$ is the same as $\boxed{/20}$

$\frac{15}{20}$ is the same as $\boxed{/4}$

$\frac{8}{10}$ is the same as $\boxed{/20}$

$\frac{1}{2}$ is the same as $\boxed{/20}$

$\frac{2}{20}$ is the same as $\boxed{/10}$

$\frac{9}{10}$ is the same as $\boxed{/20}$

Equivalent fractions

Write an equivalent fraction in each box.

$\frac{1}{2}$ = ⬚/4 = ⬚/6 = ⬚/8 = ⬚/10 = ⬚/20

$\frac{1}{4}$ = ⬚/8 = ⬚/20

$\frac{1}{5}$ = ⬚/10 = ⬚/20

$\frac{3}{4}$ = ⬚/8 = ⬚/20

$\frac{3}{5}$ = ⬚/10 = ⬚/20

$\frac{1}{3}$ = ⬚/6

$\frac{1}{10}$ = ⬚/20

$\frac{7}{10}$ = ⬚/20

Comparing fractions

You can compare fractions using signs.

> means *is greater than.*
< means *is less than.*
= means *equals.*

$\frac{1}{4}$ > $\frac{1}{10}$ $\frac{1}{10}$ < $\frac{1}{4}$ $\frac{1}{5}$ = $\frac{1}{10}$ + $\frac{1}{10}$

Compare the fractions. Write > or < or = in the boxes.

$\frac{2}{4}$ ☐ $\frac{1}{2}$ $\frac{1}{8}$ ☐ $\frac{1}{2}$

$\frac{1}{2}$ ☐ $\frac{1}{4}$ $\frac{2}{6}$ ☐ $\frac{1}{3}$

$\frac{4}{20}$ ☐ $\frac{1}{5}$ $\frac{1}{8}$ ☐ $\frac{1}{2}$

$\frac{1}{4}$ ☐ $\frac{1}{10}$ $\frac{1}{5}$ ☐ $\frac{1}{8}$

$\frac{1}{5}$ ☐ $\frac{1}{2}$ $\frac{1}{2}$ ☐ $\frac{5}{10}$

$\frac{1}{3}$ ☐ $\frac{1}{4}$ $\frac{1}{3}$ ☐ $\frac{1}{2}$

Ordering fractions

Order each set of fractions from smallest to largest.

³⁄₈   ¹⁄₄   ¹⁄₂   ¹⁄₈   ³⁄₄

¹⁄₂   ¹⁄₆   ⁵⁄₆   ¹⁄₄   ¹⁄₃

³⁄₈   ⁵⁄₈   ²⁄₈   ¹⁄₂   ¹⁄₈

³⁄₆   ¹⁄₃   ¹⁄₆   ⁵⁄₆   ²⁄₃

Dividing to find fractions

To find a fraction of a number you can divide the number by the fraction denominator.

$\frac{1}{5}$ of 20 means 20 ÷ 5.

5 is the denominator of $\frac{1}{5}$.

Write the divisions and the answers. The first one has been done for you.

$\frac{1}{4}$ of 28

| 28 ÷ 4 | = | 7 |

$\frac{1}{5}$ of 35

[   ] = [   ]

$\frac{1}{6}$ of 54

[   ] = [   ]

$\frac{1}{2}$ of 1000

[   ] = [   ]

$\frac{1}{3}$ of 27

[   ] = [   ]

$\frac{1}{4}$ of 24

[   ] = [   ]

$\frac{1}{2}$ of 80

[   ] = [   ]

$\frac{1}{10}$ of 50

[   ] = [   ]

$\frac{1}{6}$ of 42

[   ] = [   ]

$\frac{1}{8}$ of 56

[   ] = [   ]

Finding fractions

What is $\frac{3}{10}$ of 20?

To find $\frac{3}{10}$ of a number, you need to find $\frac{1}{10}$ first.

$$\frac{1}{10} \text{ of } 20 \text{ is } 20 \div 10 = 2$$

To find $\frac{3}{10}$ you multiply the answer by 3.

$$3 \times 2 = 6$$

So, $\frac{3}{10}$ of 20 is 6.

Solve these problems.

Working out

$\frac{4}{10}$ of 20 is ☐

$\frac{3}{10}$ of 50 is ☐

$\frac{7}{10}$ of 100 is ☐

$\frac{8}{10}$ of 90 is ☐

$\frac{6}{10}$ of 40 is ☐

Finding fractions

What is $\frac{3}{5}$ of 20?

To find $\frac{3}{5}$ of a number, you need to find $\frac{1}{5}$ first.

$$\frac{1}{5} \text{ of } 20 \text{ is } 20 \div 5 = 4$$

To find $\frac{3}{5}$ you multiply the answer by 3.

$$3 \times 4 = 12$$

So, $\frac{3}{5}$ of 20 is 12.

Solve these problems.

Working out

$\frac{2}{5}$ of 20 is

$\frac{3}{4}$ of 16 is

$\frac{2}{3}$ of 12 is

$\frac{3}{5}$ of 25 is

$\frac{3}{8}$ of 16 is

Answer Section

Key Stage 2 upper
Ages 9–11
Fractions

As your child finishes each page, check the answers together. Your child may like to stick a gold star at the top of each completed page as well as on the progress chart at the beginning of the book.

Eighths

When you divide something into eighths, you share it equally between eight.

Each part, or fraction, is called one eighth. You can also write it as $\frac{1}{8}$.

Two parts are two eighths or $\frac{2}{8}$.
Three parts are three eighths or $\frac{3}{8}$, and so on.

Write the fractions for the shaded squares.

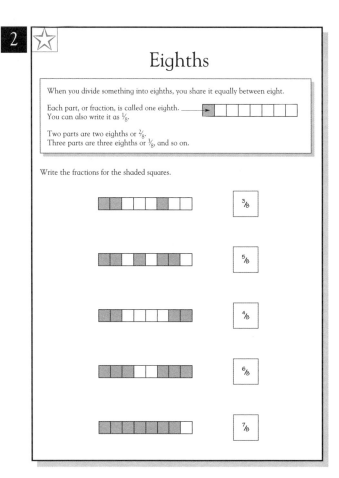

$\frac{3}{8}$

$\frac{5}{8}$

$\frac{4}{8}$

$\frac{6}{8}$

$\frac{7}{8}$

Eighths

Write the fractions for the shaded squares.

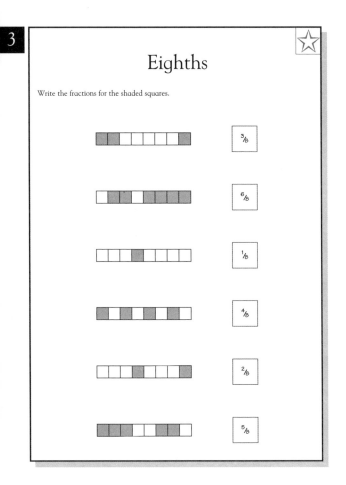

$\frac{3}{8}$

$\frac{6}{8}$

$\frac{1}{8}$

$\frac{4}{8}$

$\frac{2}{8}$

$\frac{5}{8}$

Equivalent fractions

Here are four strips of paper. They are all the same length. Each one has been cut into different fractions. You can see that some fractions are the same. For example, $\frac{1}{2}$ is the same as $\frac{2}{4}$.

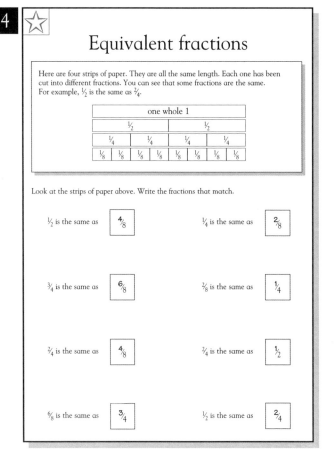

Look at the strips of paper above. Write the fractions that match.

$\frac{1}{2}$ is the same as $\boxed{\frac{4}{8}}$

$\frac{1}{4}$ is the same as $\boxed{\frac{2}{8}}$

$\frac{3}{4}$ is the same as $\boxed{\frac{6}{8}}$

$\frac{2}{8}$ is the same as $\boxed{\frac{1}{4}}$

$\frac{2}{4}$ is the same as $\boxed{\frac{4}{8}}$

$\frac{2}{4}$ is the same as $\boxed{\frac{1}{2}}$

$\frac{6}{8}$ is the same as $\boxed{\frac{3}{4}}$

$\frac{1}{2}$ is the same as $\boxed{\frac{2}{4}}$

Sixths

When you divide something into sixths, you share it equally between six.

Each part, or fraction, is called one sixth.
You can also write it as ⅙.

Two parts are two sixths or ²⁄₆.
Three parts are three sixths or ³⁄₆, and so on.

Write the fractions for the shaded squares.

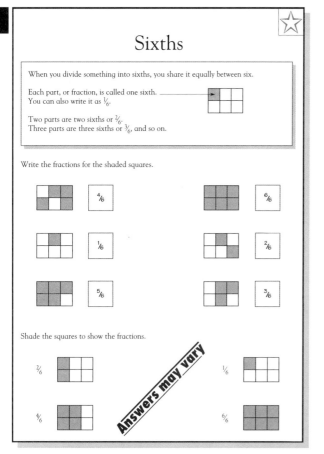

Shade the squares to show the fractions.

²⁄₆   ¹⁄₆

⁴⁄₆   ⁶⁄₆

Answers may vary

Equivalent fractions

Here are four strips of paper. They are all the same length. Each one has been cut into different fractions. You can see that some fractions are the same. For example, ½ is the same as ³⁄₆.

one whole 1					
½			½		
⅓		⅓		⅓	
⅙	⅙	⅙	⅙	⅙	⅙

Look at the strips of paper above. Write the fractions that match.

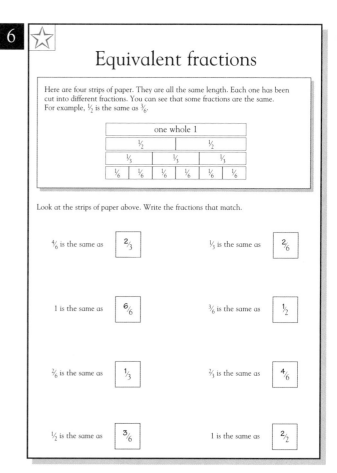

⁴⁄₆ is the same as   ²⁄₃   ⅓ is the same as   ²⁄₆

1 is the same as   ⁶⁄₆   ³⁄₆ is the same as   ½

²⁄₆ is the same as   ⅓   ²⁄₃ is the same as   ⁴⁄₆

½ is the same as   ³⁄₆   1 is the same as   ²⁄₂

Fifths

When you divide something into fifths, you share it equally between five.

Each part, or fraction, is called one fifth.
You can also write it as ⅕.

Two parts are two fifths or ²⁄₅.
Three parts are three fifths or ³⁄₅, and so on.

Write the fractions for the shaded shapes.

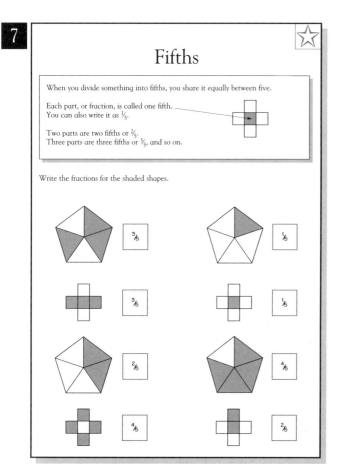

³⁄₅   ¹⁄₅

³⁄₅   ¹⁄₅

²⁄₅   ⁴⁄₅

⁴⁄₅   ²⁄₅

Tenths

When you divide something into tenths, you share it equally between ten.

Each part, or fraction, is called one tenth.
You can also write it as ¹⁄₁₀.

Two parts are two tenths or ²⁄₁₀.
Three parts are three tenths or ³⁄₁₀, and so on.

Write the fractions for the shaded squares.

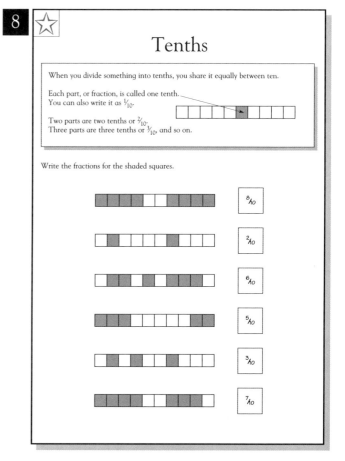

⁸⁄₁₀

²⁄₁₀

⁶⁄₁₀

⁵⁄₁₀

³⁄₁₀

⁷⁄₁₀

Twentieths

When you divide something into twentieths, you share it equally between twenty.

Each part, or fraction, is called one twentieth.
You can also write it as $\frac{1}{20}$.

Two parts are two twentieths or $\frac{2}{20}$.
Three parts are three twentieths or $\frac{3}{20}$, and so on.

Write the fractions for the shaded squares.

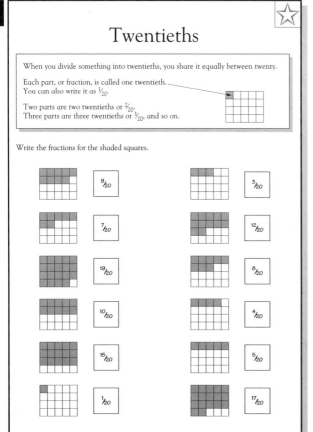

$\frac{9}{20}$

$\frac{3}{20}$

$\frac{7}{20}$

$\frac{12}{20}$

$\frac{19}{20}$

$\frac{8}{20}$

$\frac{10}{20}$

$\frac{4}{20}$

$\frac{15}{20}$

$\frac{5}{20}$

$\frac{1}{20}$

$\frac{17}{20}$

Equivalent fractions

Here are five strips of paper. They are all the same length. Each one has been cut into different fractions. You can see that some fractions are the same. For example, $\frac{1}{2}$ is the same as $\frac{5}{10}$.

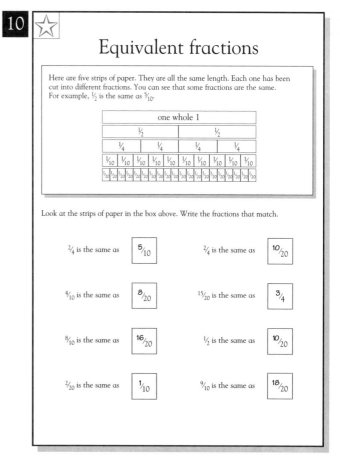

Look at the strips of paper in the box above. Write the fractions that match.

$\frac{2}{4}$ is the same as $\boxed{\frac{5}{10}}$ $\qquad$ $\frac{2}{4}$ is the same as $\boxed{\frac{10}{20}}$

$\frac{4}{10}$ is the same as $\boxed{\frac{8}{20}}$ $\qquad$ $\frac{15}{20}$ is the same as $\boxed{\frac{3}{4}}$

$\frac{8}{10}$ is the same as $\boxed{\frac{16}{20}}$ $\qquad$ $\frac{1}{2}$ is the same as $\boxed{\frac{10}{20}}$

$\frac{2}{20}$ is the same as $\boxed{\frac{1}{10}}$ $\qquad$ $\frac{9}{10}$ is the same as $\boxed{\frac{18}{20}}$

Equivalent fractions

Write an equivalent fraction in each box.

$\frac{1}{2} = \boxed{\frac{2}{4}} = \boxed{\frac{3}{6}} = \boxed{\frac{4}{8}} = \boxed{\frac{5}{10}} = \boxed{\frac{10}{20}}$

$\frac{1}{4} = \boxed{\frac{2}{8}} = \boxed{\frac{5}{20}}$

$\frac{1}{5} = \boxed{\frac{2}{10}} = \boxed{\frac{4}{20}}$

$\frac{3}{4} = \boxed{\frac{6}{8}} = \boxed{\frac{15}{20}}$

$\frac{3}{5} = \boxed{\frac{6}{10}} = \boxed{\frac{12}{20}}$

$\frac{1}{3} = \boxed{\frac{2}{6}}$

$\frac{1}{10} = \boxed{\frac{2}{20}}$

$\frac{7}{10} = \boxed{\frac{14}{20}}$

Comparing fractions

You can compare fractions using signs.

> means *is greater than*.
< means *is less than*.
= means *equals*.

$\boxed{\frac{1}{4}} > \boxed{\frac{1}{10}}$ $\qquad$ $\boxed{\frac{1}{10}} < \boxed{\frac{1}{4}}$ $\qquad$ $\boxed{\frac{1}{5}} = \boxed{\frac{1}{10}} + \boxed{\frac{1}{10}}$

Compare the fractions. Write > or < or = in the boxes.

$\frac{2}{4}$ $\boxed{=}$ $\frac{1}{2}$ $\qquad\qquad$ $\frac{1}{8}$ $\boxed{<}$ $\frac{1}{2}$

$\frac{1}{2}$ $\boxed{>}$ $\frac{1}{4}$ $\qquad\qquad$ $\frac{2}{6}$ $\boxed{=}$ $\frac{1}{3}$

$\frac{4}{20}$ $\boxed{=}$ $\frac{1}{5}$ $\qquad\qquad$ $\frac{1}{8}$ $\boxed{<}$ $\frac{1}{2}$

$\frac{1}{4}$ $\boxed{>}$ $\frac{1}{10}$ $\qquad\qquad$ $\frac{1}{5}$ $\boxed{>}$ $\frac{1}{8}$

$\frac{1}{5}$ $\boxed{<}$ $\frac{1}{2}$ $\qquad\qquad$ $\frac{1}{2}$ $\boxed{=}$ $\frac{5}{10}$

$\frac{1}{3}$ $\boxed{>}$ $\frac{1}{4}$ $\qquad\qquad$ $\frac{1}{3}$ $\boxed{<}$ $\frac{1}{2}$

13

Ordering fractions

Order each set of fractions from smallest to largest.

$\frac{3}{8}$	$\frac{1}{4}$	$\frac{1}{2}$	$\frac{1}{8}$	$\frac{3}{4}$
$\frac{1}{8}$	$\frac{1}{4}$	$\frac{3}{8}$	$\frac{1}{2}$	$\frac{3}{4}$

$\frac{1}{2}$	$\frac{1}{6}$	$\frac{5}{6}$	$\frac{1}{4}$	$\frac{1}{3}$
$\frac{1}{6}$	$\frac{1}{4}$	$\frac{1}{3}$	$\frac{1}{2}$	$\frac{5}{6}$

$\frac{3}{8}$	$\frac{5}{8}$	$\frac{2}{8}$	$\frac{1}{2}$	$\frac{1}{8}$
$\frac{1}{8}$	$\frac{2}{8}$	$\frac{3}{8}$	$\frac{1}{2}$	$\frac{5}{8}$

$\frac{3}{6}$	$\frac{1}{3}$	$\frac{1}{6}$	$\frac{5}{6}$	$\frac{2}{3}$
$\frac{1}{6}$	$\frac{1}{3}$	$\frac{3}{6}$	$\frac{2}{3}$	$\frac{5}{6}$

14

Dividing to find fractions

> To find a fraction of a number you can divide the number by the fraction denominator.
>
> $\frac{1}{5}$ of 20 means $20 \div 5$.
>
> 5 is the denominator of $\frac{1}{5}$.

Write the divisions and the answers. The first one has been done for you.

$\frac{1}{4}$ of 28
$28 \div 4$ = 7

$\frac{1}{5}$ of 35
$35 \div 5$ = 7

$\frac{1}{6}$ of 54
$54 \div 6$ = 9

$\frac{1}{2}$ of 1000
$1000 \div 2$ = 500

$\frac{1}{3}$ of 27
$27 \div 3$ = 9

$\frac{1}{4}$ of 24
$24 \div 4$ = 6

$\frac{1}{2}$ of 80
$80 \div 2$ = 40

$\frac{1}{10}$ of 50
$50 \div 10$ = 5

$\frac{1}{6}$ of 42
$42 \div 6$ = 7

$\frac{1}{8}$ of 56
$56 \div 8$ = 7

15

Finding fractions

> What is $\frac{3}{10}$ of 20?
> To find $\frac{3}{10}$ of a number, you need to find $\frac{1}{10}$ first.
>
> $\frac{1}{10}$ of 20 is $20 \div 10 = 2$
>
> To find $\frac{3}{10}$ you multiply the answer by 3.
>
> $3 \times 2 = 6$
>
> So, $\frac{3}{10}$ of 20 is 6.

Solve these problems.

Working out

$\frac{4}{10}$ of 20 is 8
$20 \div 10 = 2$
and
$4 \times 2 = 8$

$\frac{3}{10}$ of 50 is 15
$50 \div 10 = 5$
and
$3 \times 5 = 15$

$\frac{7}{10}$ of 100 is 70
$100 \div 10 = 10$
and
$7 \times 10 = 70$

$\frac{8}{10}$ of 90 is 72
$90 \div 10 = 9$
and
$8 \times 9 = 72$

$\frac{6}{10}$ of 40 is 24
$40 \div 10 = 4$
and
$6 \times 4 = 24$

16

Finding fractions

> What is $\frac{3}{5}$ of 20?
> To find $\frac{3}{5}$ of a number, you need to find $\frac{1}{5}$ first.
>
> $\frac{1}{5}$ of 20 is $20 \div 5 = 4$
>
> To find $\frac{3}{5}$ you multiply the answer by 3.
>
> $3 \times 4 = 12$
>
> So, $\frac{3}{5}$ of 20 is 12.

Solve these problems.

Working out

$\frac{2}{5}$ of 20 is 8
$20 \div 5 = 4$
and
$2 \times 4 = 8$

$\frac{3}{4}$ of 16 is 12
$16 \div 4 = 4$
and
$3 \times 4 = 12$

$\frac{2}{3}$ of 12 is 8
$12 \div 3 = 4$
and
$2 \times 4 = 8$

$\frac{3}{5}$ of 25 is 15
$25 \div 5 = 5$
and
$3 \times 5 = 15$

$\frac{3}{8}$ of 16 is 6
$16 \div 8 = 2$
and
$3 \times 2 = 6$

17 ⭐ Improper fractions

$^{17}/_{10}$ is an *improper fraction* because the numerator is larger than the denominator. You can also write $^{17}/_{10}$ as the *mixed number* $1^7/_{10}$. That is, one whole 1 made of $^{10}/_{10}$ and the remaining $^7/_{10}$.

$$^{17}/_{10} \text{ is the same as } ^{10}/_{10} \text{ and } ^7/_{10} = 1^7/_{10}$$

Convert these improper fractions to mixed numbers.

	Answer	Working out
$^{19}/_{10}$	$1^9/_{10}$	$^{19}/_{10} = ^{10}/_{10}$ and $^9/_{10}$
$^{15}/_7$	$2^1/_7$	$^{15}/_7 = ^7/_7 + ^7/_7$ and $^1/_7$
$^{10}/_3$	$3^1/_3$	$^{10}/_3 = ^3/_3 + ^3/_3 + ^3/_3$ and $^1/_3$
$^{23}/_{15}$	$1^8/_{15}$	$^{23}/_{15} = ^{15}/_{15}$ and $^8/_{15}$
$^{49}/_8$	$6^1/_8$	$^{49}/_8 = ^8/_8 + ^8/_8 + ^8/_8 + ^8/_8 + ^8/_8 + ^8/_8$ and $^1/_8$
$^{51}/_6$	$8^3/_6 = 8^1/_2$	$^{51}/_6 = ^6/_6 + ^6/_6 + ^6/_6 + ^6/_6 + ^6/_6 + ^6/_6 + ^6/_6 + ^6/_6$ and $^3/_6$

18 ⭐ Reducing or cancelling

Some fractions can be *reduced* by dividing the numerator and the denominator by a common factor.

For example, $^3/_6$ can be divided by 3 to give $^1/_2$.
This method of reducing a fraction is also called *cancelling*.

Reduce these fractions.

$^2/_4 = \boxed{^1/_2}$ $\qquad$ $^4/_{12} = \boxed{^1/_3}$

$^4/_{16} = \boxed{^2/_8 = ^1/_4}$ $\qquad$ $^{16}/_{32} = \boxed{^1/_2}$

$^5/_{20} = \boxed{^1/_4}$ $\qquad$ $^8/_{32} = \boxed{^1/_4}$

$^{100}/_{200} = \boxed{^{10}/_{20} = ^1/_2}$ $\qquad$ $^{10}/_{100} = \boxed{^1/_{10}}$

$^3/_9 = \boxed{^1/_3}$ $\qquad$ $^{200}/_{1000} = \boxed{^{20}/_{100} = ^1/_5}$

19 ⭐ Equivalent fractions

Remember: $^1/_{10} = ^{10}/_{100} = ^{100}/_{1000}$

Write the answers.

Thousandths		Hundredths		Tenths
$^{700}/_{1000}$	=	$^{70}/_{100}$	=	$^7/_{10}$
$^{300}/_{1000}$	=	$^{30}/_{100}$	=	$^3/_{10}$
$^{500}/_{1000}$	=	$^{50}/_{100}$	=	$^5/_{10}$
$^{100}/_{1000}$	=	$^{10}/_{100}$	=	$^1/_{10}$
$^{900}/_{1000}$	=	$^{90}/_{100}$	=	$^9/_{10}$
$^{200}/_{1000}$	=	$^{20}/_{100}$	=	$^2/_{10}$

Can you simplify or reduce any of the fractions in the tenths column further? If so, which ones?

$$\boxed{\text{Yes. } ^5/_{10} = ^1/_2 \text{ and } ^2/_{10} = ^1/_5}$$

20 ⭐ Growing fractions

You can grow fractions by multiplying the numerator and the denominator by the same number.

For example, multiplying both the numerator and the denominator in $^1/_2$ by 2 gives the equivalent fraction $^2/_4$. You can multiply again to grow a fraction further:

$^1/_2 \times 2 \boxed{^2/_4} \times 2 \boxed{^4/_8} \times 2 \boxed{^8/_{16}}$

Grow these fractions.

$^1/_3 \times 2 \boxed{^2/_6} \times 2 \boxed{^4/_{12}} \times 2 \boxed{^8/_{24}}$

$^1/_3 \times 3 \boxed{^3/_9} \times 3 \boxed{^9/_{27}} \times 3 \boxed{^{27}/_{81}}$

$^2/_5 \times 2 \boxed{^4/_{10}} \times 2 \boxed{^8/_{20}} \times 2 \boxed{^{16}/_{40}}$

$^2/_5 \times 3 \boxed{^6/_{15}} \times 3 \boxed{^{18}/_{45}} \times 3 \boxed{^{54}/_{135}}$

$^2/_3 \times 2 \boxed{^4/_6} \times 2 \boxed{^8/_{12}} \times 2 \boxed{^{16}/_{24}}$

$^2/_3 \times 3 \boxed{^6/_9} \times 3 \boxed{^{18}/_{27}} \times 3 \boxed{^{54}/_{81}}$

$^7/_{10} \times 2 \boxed{^{14}/_{20}} \times 2 \boxed{^{28}/_{40}} \times 2 \boxed{^{56}/_{80}}$

$^7/_{10} \times 3 \boxed{^{21}/_{30}} \times 3 \boxed{^{63}/_{90}} \times 3 \boxed{^{189}/_{270}}$

21 · Equivalent fractions

Complete this sequence up to $^{10}/_{20}$. All the fractions should be equivalent to each other.

$$\tfrac{1}{2} = \tfrac{2}{4} = \tfrac{3}{6} = \tfrac{4}{8} = \tfrac{5}{10} = \tfrac{6}{12} = \tfrac{7}{14} = \tfrac{8}{16} = \tfrac{9}{18} = \tfrac{10}{20}$$

What is happening to the numerator?

> It is increasing by one each time.

What is happening to the denominator?

> It is increasing by two each time (the 2 times table).

Complete this sequence up to $^{10}/_{30}$.

$$\tfrac{1}{3} = \tfrac{2}{6} = \tfrac{3}{9} = \tfrac{4}{12} = \tfrac{5}{15} = \tfrac{6}{18} = \tfrac{7}{21} = \tfrac{8}{24} = \tfrac{9}{27} = \tfrac{10}{30}$$

What is happening to the numerator?

> It is increasing by one each time.

What is happening to the denominator?

> It is increasing by three each time (the 3 times table).

Complete this sequence up to $^{10}/_{50}$.

$$\tfrac{1}{5} = \tfrac{2}{10} = \tfrac{3}{15} = \tfrac{4}{20} = \tfrac{5}{25} = \tfrac{6}{30} = \tfrac{7}{35} = \tfrac{8}{40} = \tfrac{9}{45} = \tfrac{10}{50}$$

What is happening to the numerator?

> It is increasing by one each time.

What is happening to the denominator?

> It is increasing by five each time (the 5 times table).

---

22 · Common denominators

The term *common denominator* means that two or more fractions have the same denominator. You can make $\tfrac{1}{2}$ and $\tfrac{3}{4}$ have a common denominator by converting $\tfrac{1}{2}$ to $\tfrac{2}{4}$ (the equivalent of $\tfrac{1}{2}$), so that both fractions have 4 as their denominator.

Convert these to fractions with a common denominator.

	Answer	Working out
$\tfrac{1}{2}\ \ \tfrac{1}{4}\ \ \tfrac{1}{8}$	$\tfrac{4}{8}\ \tfrac{2}{8}\ \tfrac{1}{8}$	$\tfrac{1}{2} = \tfrac{4}{8}$ and $\tfrac{1}{4} = \tfrac{2}{8}$
$\tfrac{1}{3}\ \ \tfrac{5}{6}$	$\tfrac{2}{6}\ \tfrac{5}{6}$	$\tfrac{1}{3} = \tfrac{2}{6}$
$\tfrac{2}{7}\ \ \tfrac{5}{14}$	$\tfrac{4}{14}\ \tfrac{5}{14}$	$\tfrac{2}{7} = \tfrac{4}{14}$
$\tfrac{1}{4}\ \ \tfrac{3}{8}\ \ \tfrac{5}{16}$	$\tfrac{4}{16}\ \tfrac{6}{16}\ \tfrac{5}{16}$	$\tfrac{1}{4} = \tfrac{4}{16}$ and $\tfrac{3}{8} = \tfrac{6}{16}$
$\tfrac{5}{6}\ \ \tfrac{5}{12}\ \ \tfrac{5}{24}$	$\tfrac{20}{24}\ \tfrac{10}{24}\ \tfrac{5}{24}$	$\tfrac{5}{6} = \tfrac{20}{24}$ and $\tfrac{5}{12} = \tfrac{10}{24}$
$\tfrac{7}{18}\ \ \tfrac{7}{36}$	$\tfrac{14}{36}\ \tfrac{7}{36}$	$\tfrac{7}{18} = \tfrac{14}{36}$

---

23 · Mixed numbers and fractions

Remember that the sign > means *is greater than* and the sign < means *is less than*.

For example, $\tfrac{17}{10} > 1\tfrac{3}{10}$ and $1\tfrac{1}{5} < 2\tfrac{2}{5}$

Write = or > or < to make these true.

			Working out
$\tfrac{10}{12}$	=	$\tfrac{5}{6}$	$\tfrac{5}{6} = \tfrac{10}{12}$ and $\tfrac{10}{12} = \tfrac{10}{12}$
$\tfrac{7}{6}$	<	$\tfrac{22}{12}$	$\tfrac{22}{12} = \tfrac{11}{6}$ and $\tfrac{7}{6} < \tfrac{11}{6}$
$5\tfrac{1}{3}$	<	$\tfrac{17}{3}$	$5\tfrac{1}{3} = \tfrac{16}{3}$ and $\tfrac{16}{3} < \tfrac{17}{3}$
$4\tfrac{5}{8}$	<	$5\tfrac{7}{8}$	$5\tfrac{7}{8} = \tfrac{47}{8}$ and $\tfrac{45}{8} < \tfrac{47}{8}$
$4\tfrac{2}{3}$	<	$\tfrac{15}{3}$	$4\tfrac{2}{3} = \tfrac{14}{3}$ and $\tfrac{14}{3} < \tfrac{15}{3}$
$1\tfrac{1}{4}$	>	$2\tfrac{1}{2}$	$2\tfrac{1}{2} = \tfrac{5}{2} = \tfrac{10}{4}$ and $1\tfrac{1}{4} > \tfrac{10}{4}$
$1\tfrac{1}{4}$	=	$\tfrac{10}{8}$	$1\tfrac{1}{4} = \tfrac{5}{4} = \tfrac{10}{8}$ and $\tfrac{10}{8} = \tfrac{10}{8}$
$\tfrac{19}{4}$	=	$4\tfrac{3}{4}$	$4\tfrac{3}{4} = \tfrac{19}{4}$ and $\tfrac{19}{4} = \tfrac{19}{4}$
$10\tfrac{1}{3}$	<	$\tfrac{34}{3}$	$10\tfrac{1}{3} = \tfrac{31}{3}$ and $\tfrac{31}{3} < \tfrac{34}{3}$
$2\tfrac{7}{8}$	>	$1\tfrac{1}{8}$	$2\tfrac{7}{8} = \tfrac{23}{8}$ and $1\tfrac{1}{8} = \tfrac{9}{8}$, $\tfrac{23}{8} > \tfrac{9}{8}$

---

24 · Number lines

Write these fractions in the right places on the number lines.

$$\tfrac{3}{4}\quad \tfrac{7}{10}\quad \tfrac{4}{5}\quad \tfrac{11}{20}\quad \tfrac{17}{20}\quad \tfrac{1}{2}\quad \tfrac{1}{4}$$

$$\tfrac{1}{3}\quad \tfrac{1}{2}\quad \tfrac{3}{10}\quad \tfrac{7}{10}\quad \tfrac{4}{5}\quad \tfrac{5}{6}\quad \tfrac{2}{3}$$

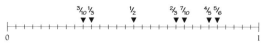

Write these improper fractions and mixed numbers in the right places on the number lines.

$$3\tfrac{1}{2}\quad 1\tfrac{2}{5}\quad 3\tfrac{1}{10}\quad \tfrac{49}{10}\quad \tfrac{9}{2}\quad 2\tfrac{3}{5}$$

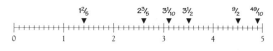

$$\tfrac{15}{2}\quad 6\tfrac{2}{3}\quad \tfrac{77}{12}\quad 8\tfrac{1}{4}\quad 9\tfrac{3}{4}\quad \tfrac{28}{3}$$

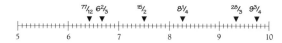

25

Ordering fractions

Write these numbers in order, with the smallest first.

$1\frac{1}{2}$ $1\frac{3}{8}$ 2 $\frac{1}{4}$ $1\frac{3}{4}$ $1\frac{5}{8}$ | $\frac{1}{4}$ $1\frac{3}{8}$ $1\frac{1}{2}$ $1\frac{5}{8}$ $1\frac{3}{4}$ 2

$2\frac{1}{10}$ $1\frac{3}{10}$ $2\frac{1}{2}$ $1\frac{1}{5}$ $1\frac{7}{10}$ | $1\frac{1}{5}$ $1\frac{3}{10}$ $1\frac{7}{10}$ $2\frac{1}{10}$ $2\frac{1}{2}$

3 $\frac{13}{3}$ $3\frac{1}{3}$ $\frac{1}{12}$ $1\frac{1}{3}$ | $\frac{1}{12}$ $1\frac{1}{3}$ 3 $3\frac{1}{3}$ $\frac{13}{3}$

Write these numbers in order, with the largest first.

$9\frac{1}{2}$ $10\frac{1}{4}$ $\frac{75}{8}$ 11 $\frac{37}{4}$ $8\frac{1}{8}$ | 11 $10\frac{1}{4}$ $8\frac{1}{8}$ $9\frac{1}{2}$ $\frac{75}{8}$ $\frac{37}{4}$

$\frac{7}{30}$ $\frac{8}{15}$ $\frac{17}{60}$ $\frac{1}{4}$ $\frac{5}{6}$ $\frac{2}{3}$ | $\frac{5}{6}$ $\frac{2}{3}$ $\frac{8}{15}$ $\frac{17}{60}$ $\frac{1}{4}$ $\frac{7}{30}$

$6\frac{1}{3}$ $\frac{6}{12}$ $1\frac{2}{3}$ $\frac{1}{3}$ $3\frac{1}{6}$ | $6\frac{1}{3}$ $3\frac{1}{6}$ $1\frac{2}{3}$ $\frac{6}{12}$ $\frac{1}{3}$

26

Halfway between fractions

What number is halfway between each of these pairs? Write the answers.
(Hint: remember common denominators.)

	Answer	Working out
$1\frac{1}{2}$ and $1\frac{3}{4}$	$1\frac{5}{8}$	$\frac{3}{2} = \frac{6}{4} = \frac{12}{8}$ and $\frac{7}{4} = \frac{14}{8}$ so $\frac{13}{8} = 1\frac{5}{8}$
$\frac{3}{8}$ and $\frac{7}{8}$	$\frac{5}{8}$	$\frac{7}{8} - \frac{3}{8} = \frac{4}{8} \div 2 = \frac{2}{8}$ so $\frac{3}{8} + \frac{2}{8} = \frac{5}{8}$
$3\frac{5}{8}$ and $3\frac{7}{8}$	$3\frac{3}{4}$	$3\frac{5}{8} = \frac{29}{8}$ and $3\frac{7}{8} = \frac{31}{8}$ so $\frac{30}{8} = \frac{15}{4} = 3\frac{3}{4}$
$5\frac{1}{4}$ and $5\frac{1}{2}$	$5\frac{3}{8}$	$5\frac{1}{4} = \frac{21}{4}$ and $5\frac{1}{2} = \frac{11}{2} = \frac{22}{4}$ $\frac{21}{4} = \frac{42}{8}$ and $\frac{22}{4} = \frac{44}{8}$ so $\frac{43}{8} = 5\frac{3}{8}$
$10\frac{1}{5}$ and $10\frac{2}{5}$	$10\frac{3}{10}$	$10\frac{1}{5} = \frac{51}{5}$ and $10\frac{2}{5} = \frac{52}{5}$ $\frac{51}{5} = \frac{102}{10}$ and $\frac{52}{5} = \frac{104}{10}$ so $\frac{103}{10} = 10\frac{3}{10}$
$5\frac{1}{3}$ and $5\frac{2}{3}$	$5\frac{1}{2}$	$5\frac{1}{3} = \frac{16}{3}$ and $5\frac{2}{3} = \frac{17}{3}$ $\frac{16}{3} = \frac{32}{6}$ and $\frac{17}{3} = \frac{34}{6}$ so $\frac{33}{6} = 5\frac{3}{6} = 5\frac{1}{2}$
$\frac{10}{12}$ and $5\frac{1}{6}$	3	$\frac{10}{12}$ and $5\frac{1}{6} = \frac{31}{6} = \frac{62}{12}$ $\frac{62}{12} - \frac{10}{12} = \frac{52}{12} \div 2 = \frac{26}{12}$ so $\frac{10}{12} + \frac{26}{12} = \frac{36}{12} = 3$

27

Halves and quarters

How many halves are there in each of these numbers?

$1\frac{1}{2}$	$10\frac{1}{2}$	$3\frac{1}{2}$	$5\frac{1}{2}$	$12\frac{1}{2}$
3	21	7	11	25

How many quarters are there in each of these numbers?

$2\frac{1}{4}$	$1\frac{3}{4}$	$5\frac{1}{2}$	$3\frac{1}{4}$	$6\frac{1}{4}$
9	7	22	13	27

How many halves and quarters are there in each of these numbers?

$15\frac{1}{2}$ $6\frac{1}{2}$ 3 9 $10\frac{1}{2}$ $13\frac{1}{2}$

Halves

31	13	6	18	21	27

Quarters

62	26	12	36	42	54

28

How many are there?

How many thirds are in the following?

	Answer	Working out
$6\frac{2}{3}$	20	$6\frac{2}{3} = \frac{20}{3}$
$5\frac{1}{3}$	16	$5\frac{1}{3} = \frac{16}{3}$

How many sixths are in the following?

	Answer	Working out
$10\frac{5}{6}$	65	$10\frac{5}{6} = \frac{65}{6}$
$3\frac{2}{3}$	22	$3\frac{2}{3} = \frac{11}{3} = \frac{22}{6}$

How many fifths are in the following?

	Answer	Working out
13	65	$13 \times 5 = 65$
$6\frac{4}{5}$	34	$6\frac{4}{5} = \frac{34}{5}$

Calculate how many of each of the fractions around the circles are contained in the numbers in the centres. Write the answers in the spaces given. Two have been done for you.

Circle 1 (centre 6): $\frac{1}{2}$ → 12, $\frac{1}{3}$ → 18, $\frac{1}{4}$ → 24, $\frac{1}{5}$ → 30, $\frac{1}{6}$ → 36

Circle 2 (centre 9): $\frac{1}{2}$ → 18, $\frac{1}{3}$ → 27, $\frac{1}{4}$ → 36, $\frac{1}{5}$ → 45, $\frac{1}{6}$ → 54

Circle 3 (centre 12): $\frac{1}{2}$ → 24, $\frac{1}{3}$ → 36, $\frac{1}{4}$ → 48, $\frac{1}{5}$ → 60, $\frac{1}{6}$ → 72

Quantities

Calculate seven tenths of each of these numbers.

	Answer	Working out
30	21	$^7/_{10} \times 30 = {}^{210}/_{10} = 21$
90	63	$^7/_{10} \times 90 = {}^{630}/_{10} = 63$
80	56	$^7/_{10} \times 80 = {}^{560}/_{10} = 56$

Methods may vary

Calculate nine hundredths of each of these numbers.

100	9	$^9/_{100} \times 100 = {}^{900}/_{100} = 9$
500	45	$^9/_{100} \times 500 = {}^{4500}/_{100} = 45$
700	63	$^9/_{100} \times 700 = {}^{6300}/_{100} = 63$

Calculate eleven hundredths of each of these numbers.

400	44	$^{11}/_{100} \times 400 = {}^{4400}/_{100} = 44$
200	22	$^{11}/_{100} \times 200 = {}^{2200}/_{100} = 22$
300	33	$^{11}/_{100} \times 300 = {}^{3300}/_{100} = 33$

Quantities and measures

Calculate $^4/_5$ of each of these.

	Answer	Working out
10 m	8 m	$^4/_5 \times 10 = {}^{40}/_5 = 8$
100 ml	80 ml	$^4/_5 \times 100 = {}^{400}/_5 = 80$
2 litres	1.6 litres	$^4/_5 \times 2 = {}^8/_5 = 1.6$

Methods may vary

Calculate $^5/_6$ of each of these.

1200 m	1000 m	$^5/_6 \times 1200 = {}^{6000}/_6 = 1000$
12 km	10 km	$^5/_6 \times 12 = {}^{60}/_6 = 10$
30 kg	25 kg	$^5/_6 \times 30 = {}^{150}/_6 = 25$

Calculate $^3/_4$ of each of these.

64 cm	48 cm	$^3/_4 \times 64 = {}^{192}/_4 = 48$
88 g	66 g	$^3/_4 \times 88 = {}^{264}/_4 = 66$
600 ml	450 ml	$^3/_4 \times 600 = {}^{1800}/_4 = 450$

Quantities and measures

Calculate $^2/_5$ of each of these.

	Answer	Working out
120p	48p	$^2/_5 \times 120 = {}^{240}/_5 = 48$
20p	8p	$^2/_5 \times 20 = {}^{40}/_5 = 8$
400p	160p	$^2/_5 \times 400 = {}^{800}/_5 = 160$

Calculate $^2/_3$ of each of these.

135 cm	90 cm	$^2/_3 \times 135 = {}^{270}/_3 = 90$
240 cm	160 cm	$^2/_3 \times 240 = {}^{480}/_3 = 160$
2100 cm	1400 cm	$^2/_3 \times 2100 = {}^{4200}/_3 = 1400$

Calculate $^3/_8$ of each of these.

168 ml	63 ml	$^3/_8 \times 168 = {}^{504}/_8 = 63$
104 g	39 g	$^3/_8 \times 104 = {}^{312}/_8 = 39$
264 cm	99 cm	$^3/_8 \times 264 = {}^{792}/_8 = 99$

Comparing shapes

There are 2 white squares to 4 shaded ones.
The shaded shape is twice as big as the white one.
The white shape is half the size of the shaded one.

Compare the shapes in each case below and write your observations.

There are 3 white squares to 6 shaded ones.
The shaded shape is twice the size of the white one.
The white shape is half the size of the shaded one.

There are 5 white squares to 10 shaded ones.
The shaded shape is twice the size of the white one.
The white shape is half the size of the shaded one.

There are 6 white triangles to 9 shaded ones.
The shaded shape is $1\frac{1}{2}$ times the size of the white one.
The white shape is $^2/_3$ times the size of the shaded one.

There are 5 white squares to 8 shaded ones.
The shaded shape is $1^3/_5$ times the size of the white one.
The white shape is $^5/_8$ times the size of the shaded one.

Improper fractions

$^{17}/_{10}$ is an *improper fraction* because the numerator is larger than the denominator. You can also write $^{17}/_{10}$ as the *mixed number* $1^{7}/_{10}$. That is, one whole 1 made of $^{10}/_{10}$ and the remaining $^{7}/_{10}$.

$^{17}/_{10}$ is the same as $^{10}/_{10}$ and $^{7}/_{10}$ = $1^{7}/_{10}$

Convert these improper fractions to mixed numbers.

	Answer	Working out
$^{19}/_{10}$		
$^{15}/_{7}$		
$^{10}/_{3}$		
$^{23}/_{15}$		
$^{49}/_{8}$		
$^{51}/_{6}$		

Reducing or cancelling

Some fractions can be *reduced* by dividing the numerator and the denominator by a common factor.

For example, $\frac{3}{6}$ can be divided by 3 to give $\frac{1}{2}$.
This method of reducing a fraction is also called *cancelling*.

Reduce these fractions.

$\frac{2}{4}$ = [ ] $\frac{4}{12}$ = [ ]

$\frac{4}{16}$ = [ ] $\frac{16}{32}$ = [ ]

$\frac{5}{20}$ = [ ] $\frac{8}{32}$ = [ ]

$\frac{100}{200}$ = [ ] $\frac{10}{100}$ = [ ]

$\frac{3}{9}$ = [ ] $\frac{200}{1000}$ = [ ]

Equivalent fractions

Remember: $\frac{1}{10} = \frac{10}{100} = \frac{100}{1000}$

Write the answers.

	Thousandths		Hundredths		Tenths
	$\frac{700}{1000}$	=		=	
	$\frac{300}{1000}$	=		=	
	$\frac{500}{1000}$	=		=	
	$\frac{100}{1000}$	=		=	
	$\frac{900}{1000}$	=		=	
	$\frac{200}{1000}$	=		=	

Can you simplify or reduce any of the fractions in the tenths column further?
If so, which ones?

Growing fractions

You can grow fractions by multiplying the numerator and the denominator by the same number.

For example, multiplying both the numerator and the denominator in $\frac{1}{2}$ by 2 gives the equivalent fraction $\frac{2}{4}$. You can multiply again to grow a fraction further:

$\frac{1}{2}$ x 2 $\boxed{\frac{2}{4}}$ x 2 $\boxed{\frac{4}{8}}$ x 2 $\boxed{\frac{8}{16}}$

Grow these fractions.

$\frac{1}{3}$ x 2 $\boxed{}$ x 2 $\boxed{}$ x 2 $\boxed{}$

$\frac{1}{3}$ x 3 $\boxed{}$ x 3 $\boxed{}$ x 3 $\boxed{}$

$\frac{2}{5}$ x 2 $\boxed{}$ x 2 $\boxed{}$ x 2 $\boxed{}$

$\frac{2}{5}$ x 3 $\boxed{}$ x 3 $\boxed{}$ x 3 $\boxed{}$

$\frac{2}{3}$ x 2 $\boxed{}$ x 2 $\boxed{}$ x 2 $\boxed{}$

$\frac{2}{3}$ x 3 $\boxed{}$ x 3 $\boxed{}$ x 3 $\boxed{}$

$\frac{7}{10}$ x 2 $\boxed{}$ x 2 $\boxed{}$ x 2 $\boxed{}$

$\frac{7}{10}$ x 3 $\boxed{}$ x 3 $\boxed{}$ x 3 $\boxed{}$

Equivalent fractions

Complete this sequence up to $^{10}/_{20}$. All the fractions should be equivalent to each other.

$\frac{1}{2} = \frac{2}{4} = \frac{3}{6} =$

What is happening to the numerator?

What is happening to the denominator?

Complete this sequence up to $^{10}/_{30}$.

$\frac{1}{3} = \frac{2}{6} = \frac{3}{9} =$

What is happening to the numerator?

What is happening to the denominator?

Complete this sequence up to $^{10}/_{50}$.

$\frac{1}{5} = \frac{2}{10} =$

What is happening to the numerator?

What is happening to the denominator?

Common denominators

The term *common denominator* means that two or more fractions have the same denominator. You can make ½ and ¾ have a common denominator by converting ½ to ²⁄₄ (the equivalent of ½), so that both fractions have 4 as their denominator.

Convert these to fractions with a common denominator.

	Answer	Working out
½ ¼ ⅛		
⅓ ⁵⁄₆		
²⁄₇ ⁵⁄₁₄		
¼ ⅜ ⁵⁄₁₆		
⅚ ⁵⁄₁₂ ⁵⁄₂₄		
⁷⁄₁₈ ⁷⁄₃₆		

Mixed numbers and fractions

Remember that the sign > means *is greater than* and the sign < means *is less than*.

For example, $^{17}\!/_{10} > 1^{3}\!/_{10}$ and $1^{1}\!/_{5} < 2^{2}\!/_{5}$

Write = or > or < to make these true.

Working out

$^{10}\!/_{12}$ ☐ $^{5}\!/_{6}$

$^{7}\!/_{6}$ ☐ $^{22}\!/_{12}$

$5^{1}\!/_{3}$ ☐ $^{17}\!/_{3}$

$^{45}\!/_{8}$ ☐ $5^{7}\!/_{8}$

$4^{2}\!/_{3}$ ☐ $^{15}\!/_{3}$

$1^{1}\!/_{4}$ ☐ $2^{1}\!/_{2}$

$1^{1}\!/_{4}$ ☐ $^{10}\!/_{8}$

$^{19}\!/_{4}$ ☐ $4^{3}\!/_{4}$

$10^{1}\!/_{3}$ ☐ $^{34}\!/_{3}$

$2^{7}\!/_{8}$ ☐ $1^{1}\!/_{8}$

Number lines

Write these fractions in the right places on the number lines.

$\frac{3}{4}$　　$\frac{7}{10}$　　$\frac{4}{5}$　　$\frac{11}{20}$　　$\frac{17}{20}$　　$\frac{1}{2}$　　$\frac{1}{4}$

$\frac{1}{3}$　　$\frac{1}{2}$　　$\frac{3}{10}$　　$\frac{7}{10}$　　$\frac{4}{5}$　　$\frac{5}{6}$　　$\frac{2}{3}$

Write these improper fractions and mixed numbers in the right places on the number lines.

$3\frac{1}{2}$　　$1\frac{2}{5}$　　$3\frac{1}{10}$　　$\frac{49}{10}$　　$\frac{9}{2}$　　$2\frac{3}{5}$

$\frac{15}{2}$　　$6\frac{2}{3}$　　$\frac{77}{12}$　　$8\frac{1}{4}$　　$9\frac{3}{4}$　　$\frac{28}{3}$

Ordering fractions

Write these numbers in order, with the smallest first.

$1\frac{1}{2}$ $1\frac{3}{8}$ 2 $\frac{1}{4}$ $1\frac{3}{4}$ $1\frac{5}{8}$

$2\frac{1}{10}$ $1\frac{3}{10}$ $2\frac{1}{2}$ $1\frac{1}{5}$ $1\frac{7}{10}$

3 $1^{3}\!\!\frac{3}{3}$ $3\frac{1}{3}$ $\frac{1}{12}$ $1\frac{1}{3}$

Write these numbers in order, with the largest first.

$9\frac{1}{2}$ $10\frac{1}{4}$ $7^{5}\!\!\frac{5}{8}$ 11 $3^{7}\!\!\frac{7}{4}$ $8^{1}\!\!\frac{1}{8}$

$\frac{7}{30}$ $\frac{8}{15}$ $\frac{17}{60}$ $\frac{1}{4}$ $\frac{5}{6}$ $\frac{2}{3}$

$6\frac{1}{3}$ $\frac{6}{12}$ $1\frac{2}{3}$ $\frac{1}{3}$ $3\frac{1}{6}$

Halfway between fractions

What number is halfway between each of these pairs? Write the answers.
(Hint: remember common denominators.)

	Answer	Working out
$1\frac{1}{2}$ and $1\frac{3}{4}$		
$\frac{3}{8}$ and $\frac{7}{8}$		
$3\frac{5}{8}$ and $3\frac{7}{8}$		
$5\frac{1}{4}$ and $5\frac{1}{2}$		
$10\frac{1}{5}$ and $10\frac{2}{5}$		
$5\frac{1}{3}$ and $5\frac{2}{3}$		
$\frac{10}{12}$ and $5\frac{1}{6}$		

Halves and quarters

How many halves are there in each of these numbers?

1½	10½	3½	5½	12½

How many quarters are there in each of these numbers?

2¼	1¾	5½	3¼	6¾

How many halves and quarters are there in each of these numbers?

| 15½ | 6½ | 3 | 9 | 10½ | 13½ |

Halves

Quarters

How many are there?

How many thirds are in the following?

	Answer	Working out

$6\frac{2}{3}$ [ ]

[ ]

$5\frac{1}{3}$ [ ]

[ ]

How many sixths are in the following?

$10\frac{5}{6}$ [ ]

[ ]

$3\frac{2}{3}$ [ ]

[ ]

How many fifths are in the following?

13 [ ]

[ ]

$6\frac{4}{5}$ [ ]

[ ]

Calculate how many of each of the fractions around the circles are contained in the numbers in the centres. Write the answers in the spaces given. Two have been done for you.

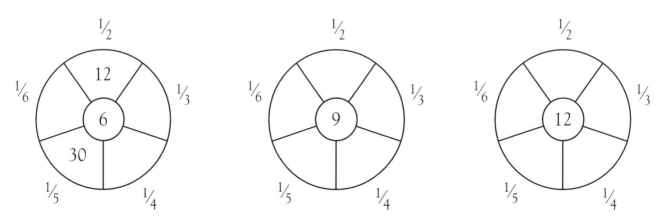

Quantities

Calculate seven tenths of each of these numbers.

	Answer	Working out
30		
90		
80		

Calculate nine hundredths of each of these numbers.

	Answer	Working out
100		
500		
700		

Calculate eleven hundredths of each of these numbers.

	Answer	Working out
400		
200		
300		

Quantities and measures

Calculate ⁴⁄₅ of each of these.

	Answer	Working out
10 m		
100 ml		
2 litres		

Calculate ⁵⁄₆ of each of these.

	Answer	Working out
1200 m		
12 km		
30 kg		

Calculate ³⁄₄ of each of these.

	Answer	Working out
64 cm		
88 g		
600 ml		

Quantities and measures

Calculate ²⁄₅ of each of these.

	Answer	Working out
120p		
20p		
400p		

Calculate ²⁄₃ of each of these.

	Answer	Working out
135 cm		
240 cm		
2100 cm		

Calculate ³⁄₈ of each of these.

	Answer	Working out
168 ml		
104 g		
264 cm		

Comparing shapes

There are 2 white squares to 4 shaded ones.
The shaded shape is twice as big as the white one.
The white shape is half the size of the shaded one.

Compare the shapes in each case below and write your observations.